Nature All Around Us

Nature All Around Us

To Observe Is to Learn, Love, and Admire

by
Robert Temple Frost

Strategic Book Publishing and Rights Co.

Copyright © 2016 Robert Temple Frost. All rights reserved.

No part of this book may be reproduced or transmitted in any form or by any means, graphic, electronic, or mechanical, including photocopying, recording, taping, or by any information storage retrieval system, without the permission, in writing, of the publisher. For more information, email support@sbpra.net, Attention: Subsidiary Rights.

Strategic Book Publishing & Rights Co., LLC
USA | Singapore
www.sbpra.com

For information about special discounts for bulk purchases, please contact Strategic Book Publishing and Rights Co. Special Sales, at bookorder@sbpra.net.

ISBN: 978-1-68181-380-6

Readers' Comments

"A gentle soul is evident in Robert Temple Frost's book of poems. They show his respect for all life and his observational skills. They are appropriate for all ages. I can see a parent including the reading of 'Ducky Caper' to a young child after a visit to a small lake or pond. As a senior citizen, I will certainly be more aware of nature all around me when I go for my walks after reading 'Morning Walk.' 'A Fish Tale' would be enjoyed by many children, those who can read it and those four- or five-year-olds who can't read yet. Best of all, I can see children drawing pictures after hearing some of these poems."

—Marlyn

"Internally smiling and thoughtful, calmed to have focused on the beauty of the detail in nature. Found myself smiling quite a bit throughout and then looking at things differently afterward. I like the title, but I also feel 'by observing, and hence learning and admiring,' we are in turn given a gift by what we see and experience."

—Jena

"Connected with and appreciative of the colorful daily moments in nature and her creatures.

Any nature lover will embrace these poems, but particularly people who appreciate the 'spirit of nature.' I enjoyed this poetry book because it focuses on Boulder wildlife. The poem 'In and Out,' about the monarch butterfly, was the one poem that gave me the tingly feeling of spirit when reading it.

"Some poems made me chuckle, others made me sad. I found them to be descriptive and could easily visualize the moments described. I also liked the questioning aspect: makes one wonder what the creature was thinking. I like that Robert captures small moments, whether it be an ant or spider or elder bug, and makes them interesting.

"These poems will certainly be enjoyed by people who love nature, but also those who are not able to be out in nature very often. These poems bring you there via the poetic words."

—Patricia

"I felt like I was with you experiencing what you so passionately and observantly describe. Your sincere awe, interest, and love for nature resounds in your written words. I felt admiration for your observation of detail in nature."

—Ama

Also by the Author

Okinawan Venture, a first novel published by Charles E. Tuttle, 1958

Scatter Radar: Space Research from the Ground, a film script written for the Wave Propagation Laboratory, National Bureau of Standards, Department of Commerce

The Knowers: First Move, a novel self-published in 1991 and still available at www.beaknower.com

The Knowers: Second Move, a literary nonfiction book written in 2010, available as a free download at www.beaknower.com

Long Trip Home: Stand Up Paddleboard Fantasy, a novel written for middle-graders in 2012, published in 2013 by Strategic Book Publishing and Rights Co. A sequel is under way.

Romance in Bloom: Sweet Sayings for One's Sweetie, a book of love poems published in 2013 by Strategic Book Publishing and Rights Co.

Contents

Preface xi

Urban Geese 1
Ducky Caper 3
Boulder Wildness 5
Morning Walk 7
Twins Remembered 9
Role Models 11
Newfound Friend 12
Envied Prize 13
False Bark 15
Wind Traveler 17
Black Ant 19
Puzzled Goose 22
Slap, Splash 24
Hideaway 27
St. Vrain Showoff 29
Downy Traveler 31
Dust Bath 32

Caterpillar	33
Concert Hall	35
No Push, No Shove	37
Mama Coon Magic	40
Last Bounce	42
Laid to Rest	44
Third Eye	46
Moose in Boulder	48
Opportunist	51
Springtime Soliloquy	52
Elder Beetle	54
In and Out	55
A Fish Tale	57
Loon Lake	60
Rest Time	62
Nature's Larder	64
No Chance to Fly	66
Joyful Victim	68
Passing Time	70
Last Bloom	71
No More	73
About the Author	75

Preface

This is a book of poems about Nature's wild ones that live in and around the city and county of Boulder, Colorado. Also included are poems about natural and geological events, some more distant from Boulder but consistent with the poetry theme to observe Nature.

In 1967 Boulder citizens voted on a referendum to buy land or development rights from landowners to keep open-space land surrounding the city forever. Ranchers could still have cattle, but they could not use their land for any other purpose. Farmers could still farm, but they sold to the city all development rights for use of their land other than farming.

Today the city of Boulder is surrounded by seventy-one square miles of open space. That's 45,440 acres! Taking the lead from the city of Boulder, electors in Boulder county adopted a similar open-space plan, as have many communities nationally, funded by voter-approved special taxes. Boulder county now has acquired 99,000 acres of open space for the purpose of keeping communities separate from each other and of stopping real estate development on critical environmental sites. All this open space includes Boulder's mountain backdrop, with peaks as high as 8,300 feet. Boulder's elevation is 5,200 feet. This wide-ranging open space gives Boulder's wild ones room to roam, to hunt, to hibernate, to be seen living and playing in many ways.

There's a robin's lilting song, a finch's melodic chirp, two squirrels chasing each other with glee around the trunk of a tree, a black bear knocking over a trash container and foraging for edibles. In the still of the night, a mountain lion attacks and kills a deer nibbling flowers in a Boulder garden. These are all signs of Nature's wild ones that live, play, and die in Boulder.

Come with me to Boulder and enjoy poems about the animals and other natural entities that make this region an extraordinary place to live and to observe Nature all around us.

Nature All Around Us

Urban Geese

I love to hear their calls
while they're still some distance away,
joyful, high-pitched barks,
conversing about plans for the day.
They're one hundred feet high,
silhouetted against a perfect blue sky.
I stopped my run on the Bobolink Trail
to watch them.
Had I called them to me
by unconscious will?
I counted eight, a family still.

They were flying in a wedge,
a usual pattern for geese,
but only a single bird was back
one position on the right—
the mama?
The other seven angled back
to the left from the leader—
a juvenile in training?

Precise spacing between each bird
was a pleasure to see.
Their wings beat in unison,
deep, powerful strokes,
light creamy-tan feathers underneath.
Their whishing sound captured their passage
with subtle ease.

I fancy they enjoy what they do each day,
commuting among fields and parks
where they eat grass and play.
The fact that it's winter
and nights are really cold
doesn't inspire them to migrate south.
They're urban geese.
Do they even know the way?

Nature All Around Us

Ducky Caper

Five mallard ducks
drifting on Boulder Creek,
along with golden leaves.
The water is so clear
I can see their feet,
tucked up in feathers.
The ducks let the current
guide their float.

In single file
they come to a flume,
a narrowed, forceful flow,
that sluices off a foot or so
into a pool below.
A drake in the lead
stretches out his neck,
dips his head into the foam,
shaking it forcefully,
spraying water off.
He makes a loud quack.

Robert Temple Frost

They circle in the eddies
like carnival riders,
along with golden leaves.
They quack and drift
from pool to pool,
each showing their joy,
as one with the flow.

Nature All Around Us

Boulder Wildness

The last quarter moon rose low in the sky.
Not enough light for me to see
what caused the noise I heard
outside the house—
sounds like no human makes.
They were thrilling and chilling
at the same time.
They caught my attention as I lay in bed
and heard them through the open window.
It started with the quick sounds of running feet,
then a scuffle, a shrill cry,
as from a terrified throat.
I heard a growl, a deep, resonant growl.
That was it, no more sounds,
and I knew what had happened.
A deer, grazing on Boulder flowers at night,
fell prey to a mountain lion,
its carcass taken away to eat—
a wildlife act that residents can value,

Robert Temple Frost

if they care to think that way.
After dark there are few boundaries
as to how Nature behaves.

Nature All Around Us

Morning Walk

Boulder Creek flows through town,
from the canyon to the west,
to the plains to the east.
It's a pleasure to enjoy
along the adjacent creek path,
which welcomes walkers, runners,
and bicyclists alike.

My wife and I are walking
on the path one summer morning,
when we see Nature all around.
We see a raven in the field with its mate,
feeding in the grass.
Pigeons perch in their high-rise nooks
under the 17th Street bridge.
We hear their youngsters' plaintive cry.
Stained sidewalk under a dead tree limb.

Prairie dogs, watching and wise,
jump upward with a jerking bark.

Robert Temple Frost

Their offspring watch their parents lead,
duck into close-by holes to hide.

Long-necked brown ducks tilt up high in a pool,
to reach down deep in the muck.
A gray bunny sits quietly under a weed.

White poppies, the last of a veritable bouquet,
a busy bee harvests their last pollen.
A turquoise beetle with a red-brown shoulder,
and two black dots meant to look like upward eyes,
roams the petal of a black-eyed Susan.

Tiny black ants in a sidewalk crack,
a dithering swarm,
anxiously attend their newly winged queen,
who is getting ready to make
her magic flight with her drones,
to mate,
before returning to her nest
for a life's work laying eggs.

We see a dusting of wildflowers—red, blue, and yellow.
We look at trout in the observatory along Boulder Creek,
the glass so dirty you can hardly see in.
We're sure the trout can hardly look out.

Twins Remembered

Two elm tree seeds
sprouted together
ten inches apart
near the end of a fence.

Each year they grew,
shading one another,
branches entwined
in a sibling embrace.
From a distance they appeared
as a single tree.

In an early spring
each tree chose
to defer to the other
the freedom to grow
without competition
for soil, for moisture,
the nutrients of life.
They both died.

Robert Temple Frost

The property owner
cut the trees down.
He left stumps
about seven feet tall.
Behind them he built
a totem—
a large, flat rock
with two stones stacked on top.

Nature All Around Us

Role Models

I saw as I approached,
at that moment in time,
two squirrels and two magpies
sharing in kind
on the grass, in a circle,
around a crab apple tree.

Each was in place at a quarter hour,
both species alternating at Nature's plate
inviting all to feed on the feast
of apples—and insects,
attracted to the hoard.

The squirrels sat upright
eating apples to the core,
while the birds picked among the overripe fruit,
finding bugs and worms to their delight.
Several minutes passed
before a diner moved apart.
The charm was broken,
and I went on my way.

Robert Temple Frost

Newfound Friend

I listened to a raven the other day.
It sat on top of a pine tree
with a lot to say.
Seven sharp calls—one followed the other.
I answered back like a practiced brother.
The raven responded with seven more calls.
I cried back with four,
the raven called back with four.
I called back with two;
the raven responded with two.
Then I knew:
The raven had accepted me as its friend.
I knew there was a nest in the old pine tree,
so high in the boughs it was hard to see.
Had the same pair of ravens been there last year?
I'm sure they were, enjoying peace, not fear.

Nature All Around Us

Envied Prize

A single raven, his beak full of roll,
sat on a telephone cable hung high on poles.
Six magpies crowded around,
jabbering the news,
that here was a feast,
if only the raven
could be made to shout,
"Get out of my face!"
and drop his treat.

The magpies took turns
darting and hovering
in front of the raven,
tail down, wings flapping,
beak and feet trying to snatch the prize
from the raven's grasp.

The raven flew from the cable
to the top of a pole.
Head bobbing, he wanted to eat his roll

by holding it with his foot
to free his beak.

Now the magpies landed on the cable
on both sides of the pole,
heckling and calling,
flapping their wings,
trying to distract him
into saying something mean.

Enough is enough—
the raven flew off through the trees,
trailed by the flock of magpies
who continued to tease.

False Bark

My wife and I left the rec center
to walk and jog on the Bobolink Trail.
As we approached the bridge
across South Boulder Creek,
we heard a yelping bark, very distinct.
Then we saw the source—
a single coyote was barking
at a black and white collie
with a woman.
Her dog was off leash.
We saw the collie leave the woman
and trot toward the coyote.
The coyote turned and jogged uphill,
looking over its shoulder, as if to say,
"Come to me so we can play."
And then we saw three other coyotes
standing together at the top of the hill.
The collie ran faster.
What was on its mind?
And then it saw there were four coyotes

one hundred feet away,
where the first one had joined the pack.
Talk about one-eightys—the collie raced back toward its
guardian, who was calling her friend to come.
At that moment a large coyote,
the alpha male of the pack,
crossed our trail two hundred feet ahead,
prepared to lead the kill.
That collie was wise to run back to its owner.
Five seconds more and it would have been too late.
Surrounded by slashing, ripping teeth,
it would have met its fate.

Nature All Around Us

Wind Traveler

I watched a spider,
as small as a dot,
traverse cross-country
on tall blades of grass.
Clinging to the blade's tip,
waving front legs to sense the wind,
it waited for a favorable breeze.

Then it leaped when it came,
drifting with ease
on its silken thread,
to reach the next blade,
a distance of two inches—
sometimes six.

If its launch failed to reach
a new height,
it quickly gathered in
the barely visible thread,
as it climbed the same blade
to try again.

Robert Temple Frost

Often it repeated,
two or three times,
before succeeding along its path.
As time passed,
it had gone quite a ways,
without dropping into the jungle
of shorter blades.

Nature All Around Us

Black Ant

Little black ant on the picnic table,
you're only about four millimeters long.
We saw you first when you were making off
with a big French bread crumb.
We could tell that you were tickled pink
to have such a prize in your jaw,
but the crumb blocked your antenna
from feeling your way.
By trying to hurry, did you think
you would get more that same day?

With all your rush you couldn't figure out,
where was the down leg to reach the ground?
You must have felt like a clown
as you kept coming back
to where you had already been.

Perplexing and puzzling, a lost ant's sin,
not to find the way you came in.

Robert Temple Frost

You were not about to change the game;
you wanted it all, that great big crumb.

A greedy gamble, but we'll hand it to you,
persistence you had
as you kept scurrying on different routes
along the side edge of the table,
and then the very low edge.
A change of wood grain
you felt through your feet.
Your memory banks flashed a recorded path.

You ran upside down along the brace to the leg.
If we thought you were running fast
on top of the table,
we couldn't believe your rapid descent to the ground.
How did you keep from falling
and at the same time run
all the way down,
holding on to your great big crumb?

When you reached the ground,
you met one of your tribe.
The good news communicated in a quick aside
pointed that ant up the same table leg
to scavenge for crumbs
like its antenna had stroked.

Nature All Around Us

What a nest hero you'll be
when, deep underground,
the storehouse is enriched
with that great big crumb.

Robert Temple Frost

Puzzled Goose

My wife and I walk along a path
to the Bobolink Trail from the rec center.
When the path divides, we wave our farewell,
as our routes are separate for another half mile.

We see each other through the trees,
a cottonwood forest along South Boulder Creek.
As we move along our separate ways,
We hear two Canada geese coming toward us.

I see the geese flying low toward the trees.
Only one goose passes in front of me.
I hear my wife call out; I look back in surprise.
A goose is standing on a six-inch tree limb.
It stretches out its neck, looking down and about.

Did the suddenness of trees confuse it,
and the limb seemed the best choice around?
Had that puzzled goose, for itself,
made things right?

Nature All Around Us

A few moments later it flies off the limb,
to join its mate in the nearby field.
What story do you think it will share?
Will it even admit its error?

Robert Temple Frost

Slap, Splash

My wife and I walk along a sidewalk path.
Green grass makes a buffer from thick bush growth,
on our right, at the edge of Boulder's Viele Lake.
We're there because a five-day rain and then flood
closed our favorite trail,
by the East Boulder rec center.

As we walk along
we hear loud, wet slaps—
slap, splash, slap, splash.
Curious as to what is making such noise,
we cross the grass
to find the end of the screening bush.
We peer around the bush at the water's edge,
and then we see the source.
A silvery fish about eighteen inches long
lies on its side in shallow water.
As we watch, it slaps its tail—
slap, splash, slap, splash—
causing the water around it

to move away from the fish
in bubbly foam.

The fish changes locations twice,
slapping the water hard at each new place.
Then the fish moves away into deeper water.
Amazingly, we then hear the same slapping again,
across the lake two hundred yards away.
Then more slapping on our side of the lake,
but farther away from us.
We count five new locations
where slapping makes the water roar.
And then it's over, no more slapping at all.
We wonder and question what it's all about.

Several days later, at Viele Lake again,
we ask a park worker who is near the lake
if he has any thoughts about the slapping.
His eyes brighten and he gives us his full attention,
with enthusiasm.
"You have witnessed a once-a-year event.
It's the carp mating process,
where the female carp has laid her eggs
in shallow water near shore.
The male carp emits sperm into the shallow water,
and then slaps the water to disperse his sperm
among the eggs.

All the carp in the lake do it at the same time, once a year.
You were lucky to be here to observe it."

There is silence between us for a brief moment or two,
as we feel pleasure learning about Nature's ways
from this naturalist,
about how carp slapping and splashing
propagates their species.

Hideaway

Sweet black birds, we think you're martins,
who usually nest in tenements square.
But you chose to be different
when a knothole you spied,
way up in a roof soffit, way up high.

It was wonderful, all that expanse,
on the old Bluebird Lodge eave.
And inside that space so secluded from view,
you both found your way to be a lodge guest, too.

We couldn't believe what we saw you do—
swoop in, pivot, and plunge up into the hole.
The fit was so tight you both had to push with your feet,
and to get all the way in, even lever with your beaks.

We watched and marveled for minutes on end,
how both of you brought stuff for a nest.
Inside we imagined there's plenty of room,
between the roof, the soffit floor, and two 2x8s.

And soon you'll have a clutch of four eggs,
to incubate, hatch, and rear your new brood.
We wondered what will happen, by and by,
when you tell them, "Now it's your day to fly."

What will your youngsters do
as they approach the spot of light
and remember what you've told them:
"Don't feel any fright"?
For days and hours before,
they'll have flapped in the nest,
to strengthen their wings
and prepare for the test.

Will that be the last time
they'll see their cozy nest,
if they can't be as agile as you two?
Will they spend future nights
out on a limb,
fated to endure the cold and the wind?

We think they'll learn,
with you encouraging them on.
Since you'll still feed them for a day or two,
they'll be free to practice and learn your ways.
They soon will become as good as you.

Nature All Around Us

St. Vrain Showoff

Pretty, leafy plant with four or five stems,
sporting fuchsia blossoms in a circle at each end,
your roots are in the sandy loam, at the water's edge.
You're the only plant like you, as far as I can see.
The seed that formed you knew
just where it wanted to be.

On an island, in a cove by a tiny, quiet bay,
where tall green reeds near you,
their feet all wet in clay,
enjoy the splashing currents
that make them wave in the wind.

You laugh at the water below your feet.
Two months ago you weren't even there,
as your parent seed, safe in the mud,
waited until the ground above
felt warm from the sun,
and then it knew it was safe to sprout.

Robert Temple Frost

The water receded to a lower level.
Then was the time for the seed to hustle,
to complete its cycle, that single seed
that has become you, so splendid indeed.

I looked at you through glasses strong,
to bring very close to view the intimate perfection
of each petal in your bloom.
And then I noticed, to my surprise,
the plant behind you also delighted my eyes.

It was pale green-gray and not too leafy,
but hanging from its almost bare arms
were wonderful shapes that equaled your charms.

They looked like large, long-legged spiders,
creamy pale yellow.
Together you two were quite a sight,
your bright colors showing off against the water,
artful spiderflowers dancing in the breeze.

Nature All Around Us

Downy Traveler

A magical conveyance floated onto my page,
a gossamer tuft of the finest black threads,
bound at the center with a matrix knot,
on which was attached a thin, triangular seed.

Silhouetted against my fingers in the sun's bright light,
I saw each thread was covered with hairs so fine,
they were hard to define
with my naked eye.

Altogether they gave more surface
to capture the breeze,
to transport its passenger with gentle ease
to some random spot.

A grass blade or weeds will snag those fine threads,
and let their passenger find a home
to nestle down
in welcoming loam.

Robert Temple Frost

Dust Bath

I watch a robin land close to me,
as I lay sunning by a tree.
She finds a hollow near the base,
removes some twigs to make clear space.

Then she lies down on the bare ground,
fluffs dirt into her feathers.
She looks at me, as calm as can be,
and rubs her head upon a wing.

She lies in the sun for a minute or two,
yawns twice to show her content,
that taking a dust bath
is her midday intent.

She stands up and shakes out her feathers.
They look pretty and shiny;
I can tell she is pleased.
Off she goes, leisure time well spent.

Nature All Around Us

Caterpillar

Tiny amber caterpillar, about half an inch long,
with a dark stripe along each side at midpoint.
I think you fell right out of a tree onto my writing pad.
I could see your determination to go your way.

When I put my pen in your path,
you tried to climb over its slippery shaft.
You fell off and reared your front half up high,
to see what in the world was making
your path so hard to try.

I see your teeny eyes down close to the paper—
no antennae, no feelers to help you decide.
So now you're confused and won't move at all.
If I touch you gently, you jerk away at a right angle.
Your back half is planted firmly on your ten tiny legs.

Now you've curled into a little ball.
I rolled you off the page onto a bare spot of dirt.

Robert Temple Frost

Within five seconds you were on your way,
soon out of sight, concealed by the tall grass
where you first wanted to be.

Nature All Around Us

Concert Hall

Little gray spider, half an inch long,
I saw you near the concert hall
as you dropped down from a tree limb
seven feet above the ground.
I was amazed at your descent,
as you created your marvelous thread,
about three feet per second,
until the ground approached your head.
It seemed clear to me you had a purpose in mind.
When you touched the ground, you quickly ran off,
not to lose any time.

The new sucker that you passed by
reached proudly upward along its parent tree's side,
leaves all shiny and new, and right beside it
was last year's stub,
nipped off a quarter inch from its parent's trunk,
all that remained from a sibling's try,
also to be a tree.

Robert Temple Frost

Inside the concert hall was another life,
not in control of where it could go.
In the dim lights of the performance in play,
a large moth fluttered back and forth
below the rafters in wide-open space,
in forlorn search for a way outside.

And so, little spider, wherever you are,
my hat's off to you for being the star,
the concert hall creature that seemed to be
fully in control of its own destiny.

Nature All Around Us

No Push, No Shove

My wife and I are at the East Boulder rec center.
As usual, we know where we will walk today,
along the creek trail on the other side of a bridge,
where a stream's whirlpool keeps foam bubbles in play.

On the way to the bridge,
we see a large turtle.
It's a foot in diameter,
almost round.
Its front claws are on the edge of the sidewalk;
it seems clear that it intends to cross.
We admire it and fuss to decide,
should we do something?
The answer is no,
so we go on our way.

A half hour later the turtle is still there.
It tucks its head down partially into its shell,
when we stoop closely to look at it.
We didn't touch it, but let it be.

Robert Temple Frost

We have never seen a turtle like this one before,
anywhere in Boulder, that's for sure.

A month later, again on our favorite trail,
a man with his dog catches our attention.
He is taking pictures with his smartphone camera.
He calls to us to come see what he is seeing.
And then we see it, too.

Tiny turtles about an inch long crawl out of a hole,
one after another, no push, no shove.
I watch one use its right flipper to wipe dirt from its eye.
The moment the turtles reach the topside ground,
they head for a pond about thirty feet away.
Its surface for days has become green with algae.
Isn't that the perfect food for its tiny new guests?

The man and his dog move away,
leaving this nature scene to us.
We stay for ten minutes more, or so,
amazed at the continuous baby turtle flow.
One after another,
no push, no shove.

The hole is located about six inches from the sidewalk,
at that same spot where, about four weeks before,
we saw that large turtle,

its front feet on the sidewalk,
as if ready to cross.

And now the baby turtles hatch.
Perfect in shape and form, they crawl out of the hole,
no push, no shove,
and they know just where to go—to the pond.

Was that big turtle we saw the mama?
Why was there no sign of fresh digging behind her?
The surrounding surface looked like all the rest,
grass and other short growth.
Yet a hole had to have been dug,
into which seventy or eighty eggs or more had been laid.
Each baby turtle emerged,
one after another,
no push, no shove.

Mama Coon Magic

Mama coon, I saw you by the curb.
You crossed the street as I approached.
Your quick trot and intense stare ahead
told me you had decided the way was clear.

Two of your youngsters were trotting behind,
as if tied to you to keep up with your pace,
but not two others that had not left the curb.

To me their little faces looked confused.
As my car lights fell upon them,
they hesitated.
They had heard you tell them,
"When I say go, we all go."

I slowed, stopped, giving them time
to make their own decision when to cross.
I saw the mother coon stop and stand up
to count her brood.
She saw me stop.

Nature All Around Us

She told her laggards to "get on the move
while considerate drivers let you pass.
The night's not over, let's make it last."

Those two scampered across
the well-lit street.
One other driver across from me,
no doubt pleased to have seen natural life,
knew by waiting a moment or two,
the mama coon's family would be intact.

Robert Temple Frost

Last Bounce

It's an awesome sight as one approaches from the east,
to see Mount Toll rising like a pyramid treat
along the Continental Divide—a fixture in space,
directing the flow of glaciers and water alike.

And it's glaciers one thinks of, envisioning the force
shearing off mountains, forming a lake
gouged deep by the glaciers' feet.
Blue Lake below was framed in stone,
its waters the color of dark green jade
reflecting the dullness of a cloudy day.

The upper cliffs show the tortured life
of freeze and thaw, like a giant maw,
fracturing the granite, letting it fall
in ringing bounces echoing off the cliffs,
until a newly freed block is stopped
by a jumble of rocks.

Climbing on the boulder field is a trip back in time,
as one observes the igneous depths of heat and stress

Nature All Around Us

stirred in the earth's bowels into a plastic state
now highly reflective with mica pate;
some with texture that swirls like half-stirred batter.

At the bottom of the slope is the virgin rock base,
worn smooth but unblemished by cracks or seams,
in contrast to the rubble that mounts to the heights.
Near the edge of the lake is a stone unlike
those that climb to the cliffs now out of sight.
It is black and bronze with a band of creamy quartz.
Maybe it was its crystals that gave it wings
on its last bounce to avoid the scree,
to fly to the water with a resonant ring.
Then it was free to lie in state
out in the open at the edge of Blue Lake.

Robert Temple Frost

Laid to Rest

Ancient ponderosa, lying on your side,
gaunt branches angling forward
from your puzzle-bark trunk.
You pointed east,
the direction you fell.
Your roots had ripped out
a mass of dirt and rocks
at your feet.

You were the largest
of your friends nearby,
exposed by yourself
to weather the winds.
And one day, a rainy day,
the ground soaking wet,
gusts from a thunderstorm
tested your strength.

The stress, the strain
as your full boughs

Nature All Around Us

bent to the wind.
Its invincible force—
the vibrations, the rocking,
the shudders—you bore,
from your upper tips
to the depth of your core.

But that day
a particularly strong blast
blew you over
with a sigh of cushioned grace,
until your under-limbs
stabbed the ground
and sheared off with loud cracks.
You eased to your side.

Your life had ended,
you knew not why.
You had spent years
reaching for the sky.

Robert Temple Frost

Third Eye

Squirrel, I see you often,
all year long,
when the sun is out.
You leave your leafy nest
to be out and about.

I watched you scamper to a tree
as I approached.
When I spoke, you jumped down
and walked toward me,
an expectant look in your eye.
With your tail over your head,
magic circles appeared—
concentric rings,
alternating dark and tawny brown.

When you flipped your tail
the pattern disappeared,
then showed again—
a protective wink.

Nature All Around Us

I felt the illusion:
you lived without fear
of any creature
that confronted your third eye.
Then, suddenly, I felt
you were not small at all.

Robert Temple Frost

Moose in Boulder

A male moose wanders into Boulder one day,
a two-year-old, its horns barely sprouted.
It spends several days wandering around the town,
before choosing North Boulder to settle down.
It grazes grass in the evening and at night,
rests during the day among the trees, out of sight.

I think the residents enjoy the sight of the moose.
They see deer often and sometimes elk.
But why should someone report the moose?
It's a new-to-Boulder animal to admire,
as it starts to graze near the sunset hour.

But somebody did call the Boulder police.
They called the State Wildlife Department.
A state game ranger arrives to locate the moose.
He radios his team and the city,
to plan the pickup of Boulder's new friend.

The crews gather and stay out of sight.
A single ranger with a tranquilizer gun

Nature All Around Us

approaches the grazing moose.
At eighty feet he lets his dart fly.
It hits the moose in the neck.
Startled, the moose stops grazing
and looks around with frightened eyes.
It tries to move,
but starts slumping to the ground.

The team arrives, carrying blankets for a gurney.
For moments they admire their prey.
While one ranger spreads a blanket on the gurney,
another ranger places a blanket on the ground.
Four rangers take the legs,
and lift the moose onto the blanket on the ground.
They tuck the legs against the body,
and wrap the blanket close.
Four rangers, all in step,
carry the moose to the gurney.
The blanket there is wrapped around the moose.
Three pairs of straps fastened to the gurney
are brought upward and buckled down.

A veterinarian with plastic gloves on his hands
takes a swipe of saliva off the partially protruding tongue.
Then he opens the jaw to peer inside with a flashlight,
to search for any signs of distress.
Satisfied, he puts the tongue back into the mouth,

and keeps it closed with a light rubber band.
The ranger van arrives; the vet waves for loading.

A crowd of residents gathers twenty feet away,
watching the moose loaded—the doors close.
A single man in the crowd asks in a loud, clear voice,
"Where will he be taken?"
The ranger answers, "Down south,
about one hundred fifty miles away into the Gunnison area,
and away from female moose."
"At least for now," the man smirks.
"When he becomes a bull, he'll go lookin'."
"I'm sure you're right," the ranger agreed politely.
"We're seeing many more young male moose
come over the Divide this summer.
Our interest is to keep them out of towns.
An adult moose can be dangerous.
Boulder is so attractive with its open-space meadows, lakes, ponds,
and growth of pines and woods.
Where else would a young moose want to be?
I'm sure we'll be back again."

Nature All Around Us

Opportunist

It was late in May, spring well started,
the flowers blooming, buds just parted.
The sun was warm, the sky clear,
when I decided to water a bush planted near
the edge of a slope, an expansive view
into the valley, the sight always seemed new.

I connected the hose and turned on the faucet,
and walked toward the bush, now a few feet away.
The stream under my thumb was not forceful—just right—
when a hummingbird darted to the nozzle.
Quick as a wink while still in flight,
she took a bath in the spray, to my wondrous delight.

Then, as I stood there, transfixed with awe,
she landed on my thumb, dipped her beak into the stream.
I couldn't believe what I experienced—
that opportunistic hummer, so willing to be seen.

Robert Temple Frost

Springtime Soliloquy

A gray day, early in May,
the downward view slips into the valley
and up to the sky, full of shrouding clouds.
Shades of gray and luminous white
tease the eye with motions and carvings.
All is quiet, with spits of rain, spats of snow,
the ground still blanketed
with late white below.

Nature caressing with tender care
the contours of a mountain horizon,
with a long, sensuous ribbon of white cloud
that mimicked the rise and fall,
so flowing and graceful,
one felt it could be touched
with gentle, undulating hand,
to caress Nature as she caressed the land.

A feeling of oneness invited
by that sweeping, varied view

Nature All Around Us

of gray upon grays, overlaying darker bands.
A symphony for the eyes, creating its own sound
in the mind of the viewer,
as spring teased winter
with humorous splendor.

Robert Temple Frost

Elder Beetle

On a knobby tree trunk exposed to the sun,
a swarm of elder beetles soaked up the rays.
There were many adults with their dark brown
orange-rimmed wings, tiny red eyes,
and two half-inch-long feelers.

But underneath them and all around
was a hatching of young,
in numbers profound.

What struck me was the fact that they varied in size,
from naked little ones, less than a millimeter long,
to all larger sizes, up to the full-winged adults.
As much as I looked, I couldn't tell where they started.
It could have been crevasses in the bark.
But now they're out in the open, and where will they go?
The temperature is close to thirty, and it's supposed to snow.

Nature All Around Us

In and Out

How can it be,
what we just saw?
An amazing feat of Nature,
and we want you to experience it with us,
as if you were here, too.

We had just bought Bev Doolittle's first color print,
an image of an Indian head resting on a bed of pebbles.
Surrounding this image in ones, twos, and groups of three
are thirteen butterflies.
They are monarchs.

During warm weather, our back door
to the outside is usually open.
As we stand back about eight feet, admiring the painting,
a butterfly comes fluttering in,
ignores us, and goes right to the painting.
It is a monarch.

The creature hovers up and down over the print,
as if communing with each painted monarch image.

Robert Temple Frost

Then it flutters out the way it came in.
We are stunned, amazed, incredulous at Nature's feat.

Could Bev Doolittle, in her artistic skill,
have imbued each monarch image
with its own organic frequency
that attracted our visitor for us to see?

Nature All Around Us

A Fish Tale

The aquarium is very attractive,
placed where the traffic goes by.
I see it often when I'm passing
on my way to the pool to swim.

One day a fish drew my attention
when he raised his spiny back fin.
He was a blue gill, with dark bluish black sheen.
I counted three smaller fish and a sucker,
its large mouth open for effective use,
cleaning coral, pebbles, even the sides
with jerky little movements
between sinuous glides.

I like the notion that organic life is as one,
so I decided to name that bigger fish Juan.
He was alone in the center,
with open space all around.
I approached the tank thinking his name.
When I talked to him, could he hear my sound?

Robert Temple Frost

"Oh, what a pretty fish you are.
Do you enjoy what you do each day?"
Juan looked at me with his movable eyes,
chased away a smaller fish that came too near.
He returned to the glass and looked at me again.
He seemed pleased; did he think he was my peer?

Near the glass, I opened my mouth and fingers,
then closed them quickly as Juan watched my act.
He opened his mouth wide,
and raised the spiny fin on his back.
I did it again and he responded as before.
I knew then our friendship would not lack.

Do fish have emotions when they're talked to?
With Juan it was clear that he did,
as he enjoyed our visits and greeted me.
But as the weeks went by, I noticed something new:
Juan was changing color to a mottled golden hue.

His color changed in just a few days,
and then his behavior changed, too.
Juan no longer was out in the middle;
he hid out among the coral and fern.
I had a sense that our every-other-day visit
had become too stressful.

Nature All Around Us

Did Juan interpret my gestures
as commands for him to obey?
Did the fact that a human was talking to him
stress my little fish friend so he didn't feel okay?
I decided to visit him only on Saturday,
to see if his withdrawal mode would allay.

This did seem to help,
as sometimes he would be back
in the open, as before,
but then as I approached, he would dart away,
showing reluctance to interact anymore.

I felt bad but thought I understood his mood.
He found it stressful to keep doing things new.
The weeks passed with little change,
but one day something amazing occurred.
Juan was out in the center as I approached.
When he swam to the glass in open greeting,
I told him I was happy to see him again,
and hoped his behavior wasn't something fleeting.

Then a little fish swam close to say "Hello," too.
Instantly, Juan herded that fish into a circle,
He stayed on the outside, keeping the circle tight.
They went around and around, many times and more.
The little fish looked at me, expressing worry.
Juan wasn't mean—just deliberate in his chore.

Robert Temple Frost

Loon Lake

It's called Bison Lake on the Flat Tops Plateau.
My wife and I knew better; we ought to have known.
We only saw loons on its vast expanse.
No other ducks were taking a chance.
Black with white on body and wings,
loons are visible as they practice their routine,
diving underwater for half minutes at a time.
They catch their food to stay in their prime.

We watched brown-feathered juveniles learn the art
while the parents looked on as they dived on their mark,
soon to bob up many feet away
on the parents' other side, as if in play.

Early in the morning the loons were on the ground.
The lake was a mirror; we didn't hear a sound.
Then the loons awakened and walked out of their park.
They entered the water with a raspy, trolling bark.
Their disturbance caused ripples to come our way.

Nature All Around Us

The mirror clarity was lost for the day.
The loons toured and dived and flew so low
their wing tips wrote hyphens in the water with reflective
 glow.

Robert Temple Frost

Rest Time

We love our home on Uni Hill, not far from open spaces.
We feel blessed when we can see a variety of wild faces—
squirrels, raccoons, skunks, fox, bear, often deer.
The latter, it's their pellets leaving evidence they were near.

Our bathroom window looks east onto a narrow street.
The far curb and pine trees are less than a hundred feet.
On a cold night in January, the street was glazed in ice.
My wife arose at two a.m. and looked out the window, twice.

The window was partially open; a full moon lit the scene.
She saw two bucks bedded down on fresh snow so clean.
A doe jumped over a low stone wall behind the second deer,
and walked out into the open showing no sign of fear.

Her insistent hand on my shoulder awakened me from my
    dream.
"Robert! Robert! Wake up! Come see what I have seen!"
Her voice was low; I struggled to waken.

Nature All Around Us

I went to the window with my kitty, then all the space was
 taken.

The two bucks were resting under upswept branches of pine.
The moonlight glistened on the larger buck's ten antler tines.
Their silhouettes and proud heads were in clear relief.
We could sense their comfort, enjoying early morning peace.

As we watched them for several minutes, we felt they knew,
when they turned their heads to look our way, too.
Human voices startled us up the street, a block away.
Both bucks turned to listen and to watch the coming sashay.

A car came down the street, going pretty fast.
Two young men hung onto the rear bumper as the car drove
 past,
yelling and screaming while sliding on their boots.
About the slumbers of the neighborhood they didn't give a
 hoot.

They passed in a moment, and we were surprised to see
both bucks and the doe not disturbed by the shouting and
 the glee.
We thought the deer knew they hadn't been seen.
The antics of humans only briefly interrupted their quiet
 scene.

Robert Temple Frost

Nature's Larder

My wife and I took an early morning hike.
The old mine, our goal, was still out of sight
when the sun finally cleared the ridge with ease,
golden reflectivity showed us a frieze
of seedpods—all that was left
of blooms that had performed their best.

We saw each plant as a personality,
offering its children with generosity,
to a breeze or an animal passing by,
to scatter, to snag a seed and take it away,
possibly to germinate on some future day.

But, for our moment, the seeds were still there,
waiting for us to admire and find them fair.
They were certainly different,
and I'll tell you how,
as to Nature's dainty elegance
we did bow.

Nature All Around Us

We saw a simple stalk,
where each seed was like a pea
dangling on a delicate stem.
We saw purple blossoms
in their last days of bloom,
where the lowest flowers on each plant
had turned into puffballs ready to fly
the moment a quick breeze passed them by.

We saw a bush that glowed
with a silvery-gold sheen.
The seeds displayed silky strands
shaped like a hook
that directed the breeze
to suck it from its socket.

A golden-tan plant had formed a seed,
presenting fibers of the softest touch,
like an artist's finest camel's-hair brush.

When most of the seeds are on the ground,
we know they'll be food for creatures all around,
to gather them, to hide them,
to eat them right away.
The seeds ending summer
will keep famine at bay.

Robert Temple Frost

No Chance to Fly

Poor little dead bird floating in the pool,
you are only half feathered,
many days from flight.
Was there one too many faces
for your parents to feed,
as they searched for food
for all your nest-mates' needs?

Did you get pushed out of your nest
and fall below in fright?
Or, in the frantic struggle
to be the closest beak to see,
did you flutter and chirp
too close to the edge,
and fall out of the tree?

No doubt when you hit the water
you were panicked and afraid.
Did your mother fly by in her instinct to save?
Did you cry out to her,

Nature All Around Us

and flutter your wetted short feathers?
If no one saw, no one could save.
You died in your wet and lonely grave.

Robert Temple Frost

Joyful Victim

In cities and towns, Nature is alive
with seasonal birds, skunks, and magpies.
But among them all, the ones I love best are squirrels.
I saw one argue with a jay over a handful of peanuts on a tray.
I saw two sit upright with two magpies, eating apples to the
    core.
I've seen their leafy nests wave in a winter breeze,
as the squirrel inside hugged its tail in comfort and ease.

They have few predators—only joy with life.
They chase each other around the trunks of trees,
as their magical claws let them run horizontally.
One thing is certain: cars are their risk,
as a careless crossing can end in a squish.

You've seen them, I've seen them,
flattened, dried-out husks,
waiting for night scavengers as soon as it's dusk.

One day I was driving at a cautious speed,
as I watched a squirrel ahead about to cross.

Nature All Around Us

A black SUV drove toward me, too fast.
The driver didn't see the squirrel dart into its path.
The squirrel almost made it
as it disappeared from my sight,
but its hind legs were trailing
as it ran in full flight—
they were crushed.
I saw that squirrel struggle,
its upper body straining to be erect,
dragging itself to the nearby curb.
I slowed to watch its front claws grasping for a grip
to pull itself up and into the weeds,
no longer able to frolic in the trees.
I felt that squirrel suffer—and cry,
as it waited to die—joyful victim.

Robert Temple Frost

Passing Time

Pretty little butterfly, a surprise for the season.
Late-blooming flowers give you good reason
to enjoy sweet nectar you suck from the bloom,
as your uncoiled tongue slips into each tube.

You land once on the edge of a barrel
savoring the sweetness before going for more.
Your beautiful wings move gently,
you're alert to fly.
If anything threatens,
you'll dart to the sky.

You've done your best,
with your eggs laid away.
So each day of sun and mild nights
have extended your stay.

It's good there are late flowers
to succor your needs.
But someday soon, on a freezing perch up high,
you'll fold your wings—and prepare to die.

Nature All Around Us

Last Bloom

It's a sunny day in October, Indian Summer is here.
The zinnias, petunias, long-lasting flowers,
all hold their heads high
despite the chilly night air.

I come to a bush along the way,
one of many of its kind,
dark green, small leaves with yellow blossoms,
that start to bloom around the middle of June.

It's a bush I see often in the lower mountains,
a foothills bush, a delightful charm.
Each branch presents buds of varying size,
each bud blooming at its appropriate time.

The bush I see had run its course,
the old blooms all shriveled and dry.
What caught my eye was a single bright flower,
there were no others on the entire bower.

Robert Temple Frost

I pause – and nod my head with feeling,
that last bloom was intent for seeing.

No More

Remembering the September 12, 2013, Boulder Creek Flood

Poor little prairie dogs,
getting furry for the season.
Little did you know
what was about to happen.

The rain started,
a day at a time, then two, then three.
That was not so bad.
But, on that fourth day,
it rained nine inches.

The ground, soaked
from previous wet,
could absorb no more,
and the creek spilled over
your colony of holes,
a foot, or two, or three.

Robert Temple Frost

And there you were,
all of you,
in your deep-down burrows,
nowhere else to go,
no way to breathe,
as the water flooded into your burrows,
and killed you all with ease.

Bless you, little puppies,
I enjoyed seeing you romp and play,
and stand so tall, and bark with glee,
to celebrate your living for all to see.

But no more—
your colony is now a wasteland
covered with sand and debris.

About the Author

Robert was born in 1930 and raised in Denver and Colorado Springs, Colorado. He earned a business degree from the University of Colorado. He joined the US Air Force during the Korean War and served a tour on Okinawa as a petroleum officer. In 1957 Robert was employed by the Department of Commerce in Boulder, Colorado, and served as business manager for research laboratories before completing a thirty-six-year federal career. He retired in 1990 and self-published his second novel, *The KNOWERS: First Move*. In this novel Robert expresses his views about the need for political changes, exploring the possibilities of a new political party and candidates committed to resolve political and social dysfunctions. The 322-page novel has a strong new consciousness and spirituality theme. Go to Robert's website, beaknower.com, to review the book and reviewers' comments and to order the book. You will find that a nonfiction sequel, *The KNOWERS: Second Move*, is available to read and/or download free.

Robert is also a published poet. His book, *Romance in Bloom: Sweet Sayings for One's Sweetie*, was published in 2013 and is available to order through his publisher's website, sbpra.com/RobertTempleFrost. Robert is also working on a sequel to his novel *Long Trip Home: Stand Up Paddleboard Fantasy*.

Review Requested:

If you loved this book, would you please provide a review at Amazon.com?

Made in the USA
Monee, IL
03 May 2026